GW00689799

The Chipmunk

A guide to selection, housing, care,

nutrition, behaviour, health, breeding,

species and colours

Content

Foreword

The chipmunk is a squirrel species which has been kept as a pet by enthusiasts for many years. Although one can find more and more chipmunks in pet shops, it is still very difficult to find information about this species, which is why About Pets dedicates this book to these lovely pets.

The book you are holding in your hands has been written to provide you with the basic information you need to keep chipmunks as pets in a responsible manner. This book is not an in-depth encyclopaedia for advanced enthusiasts or breeders. The 64 pages of this book do not offer enough space for this.

Besides general topics, such as origin, purchase, feeding, housing, care and reproduction, we also deal with a number of illnesses. Furthermore, we pay attention to a number of associations which focus on these special pets and where you can get more information about chipmunks.

About Pets

A Publication of About Pets.

ISBN 1852792094
First printing
September 2005

Original title: *De boeroendoek*
© 1998 - 2005 Welzo Media Productions bv,
About Pets,
Warffum, the Netherlands
www.aboutpets.info

Photos: Peter Verberne,
Joop Lanting, T. Spielmans,
W. Toonen, Kingdom books and Rob Dekker

Printed in China through Printworks Int.Ltd.

In general

Their playful character, their athletic ability and their friendly squirrel appearance have made these animals very popular with humans.

Most squirrels are very difficult to keep in captivity. The European Red Squirrel (*Sciurus vulgarus*), which can be found in our woods, is also a protected species. You may only keep it as a pet if you can prove that it was born in captivity.

The Asian Chipmunk (*Eutamias sibiricus*) is a pretty, playful squirrel, which may be kept as a pet in the UK. A chipmunk makes an ideal pet, although it does have its demands when it comes to housing, feeding and care. If you fulfil these demands, you will have an active, attractive and colourful companion.

Chipmunks are not yet very well known in the pet world, as they are fairly expensive and need quite a

lot of space, at least in comparison to other, smaller rodents, such as gerbils and hamsters. As breeding of pet chimunks is becoming more common and easier, the number of animals for sale will increase and the price reduce. They will probably never be really cheap, though, as squirrels give birth to no more than ten young per year. The fact that chipmunks are expensive prevents them from being bought on the spur of the moment and without further thought.

Exotic mammals
In comparison to hamsters and mice, chipmunks are exotic mammals and must be treated as such. 'Exotic' conjures up images of far-away, sunny places, but it means nothing more than foreign,

not from our region. So any mammals that do not originate in our region are therefore exotic.

Exotic mammals have not yet been fully domesticated. This means that they are not yet as adapted to life in captivity as the cat, guinea pig, rabbit, dog or hamster. Exotic mammals therefore have their own, sometimes quite challenging, demands when it comes to care, feeding and housing. These demands differ from animal to animal. If you plan to keep one or more exotic pets, you have to make sure that you get proper information beforehand.

The chipmunk

Some confusion exists when naming this furry little creature. In English, it is called Chipmunk, Asian Chipmunk, or Asiatic Ground Squirrel. As most languages also have their own names for these striped squirrels, you will probably end up with hundreds of different names throughout the world. The Latin name *Eutamias sibiricus* is therefore the only reliable one. Scientists and fanciers from all over the world will know which animal is meant with this name, whereas they probably won't know what a 'chipmunk' is. As using the Latin name would make reading this book more difficult, we have chosen to use the English name, chipmunk.

The Asian Chipmunk, together with fifteen other species, belongs to the *Eutamias* family. They are closely related to the North American *Tamias* family. This includes six species of pouched squirrels, also known as 'chipmunks'.

Two very well known examples of this species are Walt Disney's 'Chip 'n' Dale'.

'Chipmunk' is a collective name for all striped ground squirrels. The Asiatic Ground Squirrel is therefore a chipmunk, just as the Eastern Chipmunk (*Tamias striatus*) is.

Until recently, chipmunks were divided into two families: *Eutamias* were the species from Northwest America and Eurasia, while *Tamias* were those from Northeast America. Most scientists still make this distinction. Recent scientific research, however, shows that these families are so closely related that such a distinction is actually not correct.

Chip 'n' Dale
© Walt Disney

In contrast to many other animals, chipmunks climb down with their head first.

It is not quite certain where the name chipmunk comes from. A lot of people believe that it derived from the 'chip-chip' sound the ground squirrels make. It is, however, more probable that the name has developed from the Native American word 'achiitaman' or 'cheetaman'. It means 'first' and is supposed to indicate how chipmunks descend from trees: head first.

This book deals with the Asian Chipmunk, as it is the squirrel most commonly kept as a pet in this country. The care of other chipmunks is not really different to that of the Asian Chipmunk. Most chipmunks on sale here have originated in Korea or Siberia. If you are offered an anmal under the name of chipmunk or ground squirrel, it is almost certainly an Asian Chipmunk. It is not very likely that you will find an American Chipmunk here.

Origin

The Asian Chipmunk is originally a Siberian squirrel. The animal adapted so well to its environment, that it slowly spread south and west. It is now found in the whole of Siberia and Russia, in big parts of Northern China, the whole of Mongolia and Korea, parts of Japan, and in Finland. The chipmunk's habitat is therefore vast and has many different climates: from ice-cold Siberian winters to the continental climate of China's plateaus and the sub-tropical woods of Korea. So it is hardly surprising that the chipmunk can survive in our climate without too much trouble. Groups of chipmunks have been spotted in the wild in Holland, France, Germany and Austria.

Bringing a foreign animal species into the British environment can displace native species and cause other damage. The rabbit pests, which cause problems in Australia quite regularly, are a good example.

Appearance

The chipmunk has big pouches and black and light stripes on the back and flanks of its slim body. The chipmunk's fur is short, soft and light brown to golden-red in colour. An obvious characteristic is the five black stripes on its back. The stripes alternate with two white and two light brown stripes. The stripes carry on into the beautiful bushy tail. The animal is white underneath. The colour of its coat can vary. Some chipmunks are greyish brown, others are a deep, reddish brown. Whatever colour, any animal kept outside will have a thicker coat and therefore stronger colours.

Sub-species

Chipmunks are ground animals, but they also forage for food in trees. They can therefore be regarded as something between the real tree squirrels, such as the Red Squirrel (*Sciurus vulgarus*) and the Grey Squirrel (*Sciurus carolinensis*) and the real ground squirrels, such as the Black-tailed Prairiedog (*Cynomys ludovicanus*), the European Souslik (*Citellus citellus*) and the Spotted Souslik (*Citellus soeslicus*).

Natural coloured chipmunk

Over the last years, colour mutations developed, such as this lighter variety. There are also completely white chipmunks.

Eurasian chipmunks are quite often from different sub-species, but all from the same species. Two sub-species are kept in Western Europe, the South Korean *Eutamias sibiricus barberi* and the Eastern Siberian/ Japanese sub-species *Eutamias sibiricus lineatus*. The third part of the Latin name indicates the sub-species, here *barberi* and *lineatus*. Crossing these two sub-species has led to a population of animals in the UK, which may have characteristics of either one of the sub-species.

Teeth

A chipmunk is a true rodent and does its name justice: it gnaws. 'Rodent' comes from the Latin word 'roere', which means 'to gnaw'. A rodent is so good at its job because of the unusual combination of incisors and molars in its mouth.

The sharp incisors make it possible for the chipmunk to chew through virtually anything. The molars in the back of the mouth grind the food down. A gap called 'diostema' is located between the incisors and the molars. This gap makes it possible for the jaws to close behind the incisors. This means that rodents (such as chipmunks and hamsters) can carry on gnawing while they swallow only selected bits or keep them in their pouches.

A rodent's incisors have to work very hard and therefore grind down quite quickly. They grow continuously. It is therefore very important that the incisors of the top and lower jaw fit onto each other properly. If this is not the case, then the teeth carry on growing and so-called 'elephant's teeth' develop. The animal will no longer be able to eat (also see chapter 'Your chipmunk's health').

How it digests its food

Rodents are usually omnivores (they eat anything). Rodents also eat bits of plants such as seeds, roots, twigs, leaves and fruit. They don't have an extensive digestive system adapted to digesting plant food, such as herbivores (plant-eaters) have. In the case of rodents, bacteria in the intestines take on this task. These bacteria contain cellulase, i.e. enzymes that break up cellulose. They are situated in the 'caecal sacs' of the large intestine, which looks like the human appendix.

Sexing

There is no obvious difference in appearance between male and female chipmunks. To determine its sex, you have to look under the animal's tail. Most chipmunks are very reluctant to be picked up. It is therefore easiest to look while the animal

is walking over a mesh or glass floor. You can also see its sex when the chipmunk is hanging onto mesh.

As with all rodents, you can determine its gender by looking at the distance between the anal opening and the genital opening. It is approximately five millimetres on male chipmunks, but less on females. The difference is more obvious in the mating season. The male's testicles drop into the scrotum, which makes the latter appear bigger and darker.

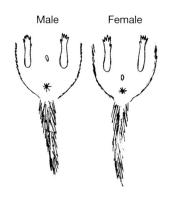

Male   Female

Buying your chipmunk

The first meeting with a squirrel, and certainly also with a chipmunk, is normally love at first sight: a cute animal looks at you from behind the bars with an inquisitive and bright face.

This look makes most animal lovers melt like butter. It also happens quite often that someone goes to buy cat food, finds himself eye to eye with a squirrel, falls in love and buys the animal. This is what you call an 'impulse buy'. Buying a pet on the spur of the moment is the worst thing you can do for the animal, but also for yourself.

Whenever you plan to buy a pet (whether it is large or small), it is important that you find out what type of animal it is exactly. Is it active by day or by night? What and how often does it need to eat? How much space does it need? How often do you need to clean its cage?

One or more?

How many chipmunks should you buy, and at which age and of which sex? This depends on various things. Chipmunks live in colonies, but have their own territory within the group. They therefore actually live alone and only meet up to mate.
As chipmunks are being bred more often in captivity nowadays, they are becoming more sociable towards others of their kind, and they can sometimes be kept in pairs.

You still need to be careful with keeping several chipmunks in one cage. You cannot tell by looking at the animal how long its family has been domesticated. An imported animal will certainly massacre its roommates at the right moment.

Even two animals, which have been living together peacefully for years, can suddenly start a fight. There are also periods when these animals are less sociable towards each other. A pregnant female can be very aggressive towards a male; she will also be quite touchy shortly after giving birth. Autumn is also a time when you need to watch out for fights. If you still want to keep two or more animals in one cage, take care of the following:

- The animals need plenty of room, so that they can flee from each other. Plan one cubic metre per animal.
- Make sure that they have enough nesting logs or other shelter. Put in more logs than animals.
- Always be alert. A bit of squabbling is ok, but prevent casualties.
- Give plenty of food, preferably spread over several spots in the cage. This prevents fights over food.

There are plenty of examples of chipmunks that live together quite peacefully. This is a bonus if you want young. You then need at least one male and one female. Be extra careful when sexing the animals. It would not be the first time that a planned mating has not happened, because someone did not look under the animals' tails properly.

If you plan to breed, get two non-related chipmunks. It is very important to prevent in-breeding. If two animals from one family mate, problems can occur, such as weak and malformed young. This does not normally happen in the first generation, but it will after a few, if no outside 'blood' is introduced.

If you want to buy a couple to breed, do not buy one that is too old, fully grown and has already had young once or twice. Do not buy animals over four years of age. There is furthermore no guarantee that any two animals will actually reproduce.

Where to buy
There are various ways to buy a chipmunk. But buy responsibly!

The pet shop
Chipmunks are increasingly on sale in pet shops, especially in cities, although they don't really belong there. Pets are often bought on the spur of the moment and people are not always supplied with the right information. There are also plenty of unpleasant images of neurotic squirrels in small birdcages, injured animals and others that are being fed completely wrongly. These chipmunks are also often from 'the trade': imported animals, of which a large number dies on the way to this country due to bad treatment.

There are also pet shops that get their animals from fanciers or import them in a responsible manner. They can provide you with the right information, but, sadly, they are not very common. A badly run shop will have the following characteristics: dirty, small cages without water and food, ill animals and an ignorant salesperson, who can sometimes (unfortunately) hide his ignorance behind nice talk.

The fancier
Quite a number of people breed chipmunks in this country. These animals are normally used to humans and to life in captivity.

Most fanciers can also give you vital, useful advice regarding feeding, housing and care.

These fanciers are not always easy to find. A lot of them can be found on the internet. You can find information on websites on page 62 of this book.

Things to watch out for
If you want to buy a chipmunk as a pet, preferably buy an animal that is between eight and sixteen weeks old. Animals older than sixteen weeks will not become totally tame. Also never buy an animal that is younger than eight weeks: A chipmunk needs its mother's milk and warmth too.

Whichever squirrel, and at whatever age, you buy, always make sure that it is lively, has shiny fur and clear eyes. Also look out for scars and other wounds. Check that the animal moves properly and does not have

any malformations. Make sure that its tail is bushy and intact. Animals with injuries are normally old(er) or imported. They may also be hooligans.

It is inadvisable to buy a chipmunk that is aggressive towards humans and others of its kind. Buy several animals at the same time, where possible. If you buy one animal later, you will risk that they will not accept each other. In this case, try to negotiate with the vendor that you can bring the chipmunk back if it does not 'click'. This entails that the animal is still intact after a failed introduction, of course!

Giving away young chipmunks

Keeping chipmunks can become addictive quite quickly. Many fanciers cannot bring themselves to sell, swap or give away their young. There will come a point, however, where you can no longer keep all the animals. There are various places to take young (and old) animals. You can sell them to a pet shop, but then you won't know where they will end up. Make sure you find a responsible pet shop, and supply them with plenty of information.

You can also sell your animals to individuals. This can happen via the internet, or via ads in the papers, or, preferably, you can sell them to acquaintances. Here, too, you have to give their new owners sufficient information.

Never set an animal free in the wild! Many pets won't survive, although the chipmunk has a slightly higher chance than others. Animals released in the wild can cause a lot of damage to the environment. They do not have natural enemies here and may displace native species.

Catching a chipmunk

Whenever you need to catch a chipmunk, for whatever reason, it can cause a fair bit of trouble. A squirrel is very quick and catching it puts the animal under a lot of stress. It is better to lure your chipmunk into a 'trap' and to transport it within this. Put a box into one corner of the cage some time in advance, and fill it with some treats. Make sure that you can close the box from outside the cage. Let the animal get used to the box without pressure. It will then be easy to catch.

If the animal has to be caught straight away, use a net. Wear gloves, as a chipmunk can bite you very badly through a net.

Vulnerable tail

The tail is one of the chipmunk's most vulnerable parts. Never catch the animal by grabbing its tail. The fur will come off, and the animal will run away bleeding. This is a leftover from life in the wild: it gives the chipmunk a chance against predators. If a wild cat wants to grab it, the detachable tail guarantees a 'second chance'.

Transport

When transporting a chipmunk, use a suitable, dark box or cage. This will calm the animal. Never transport rodents in cartons! Be aware of high temperatures in parked cars and of toxic exhaust fumes. Try to keep the travel time to a minimum. The whole undertaking is nerve-wrecking enough.

Feeding your chipmunk

Chipmunks are active all day long. They therefore also want to eat continuously. This is why they really need access to food all the time.

As a chipmunk hoards food, you do not have to feed it every day. You need to allow the animal to build up stocks, though, and don't throw the food out when cleaning their cage.

Animals have their favourite food too. They would like to eat it every day, of course, but that is not good for their health. A one-sided diet will lead to illnesses over time. Sunflower seeds, for example, are a tasty treat for rodents, but they contain a lot of fat. If you give your chipmunk a bowl of mixed food with sunflower seeds, it will first eat these and leave the rest until it is hungry again. It will then eat the other seeds. So never feed too many sunflower seeds or other fattening food.

The above can only be a general guideline. There are animals that really do not like certain things. This depends on the individual. Chipmunks that hibernate also have to prepare themselves. They do this by stocking up, whether in body fat deposits, hoards of food in their nest or burrow, or a combination of both. You can read more about hibernation in the chapter 'Behaviour'. Chipmunks will also eat certain things at a certain time of the year, and not at another time.

It is therefore impossible to describe a menu here that applies to each and every chipmunk. The suitability of its diet depends on the individual animal. You have to create a healthy menu for your chipmunk(s) yourself. The most important thing is to make it as well balanced as possible. This means that you cannot feed your squirrel only acorns in October, just because they happen to be falling off the trees en masse at that time. A chipmunk needs seeds, nuts, fruit and possibly animal nutrients in similar quantities throughout the year. The only exception is when it prepares for hibernation. It will then need more fattening food to be able to build up reserves.

Main feed

In the past, chipmunks and other seed- and nut-eating squirrels were given mixed rodent food as their principal diet. This food was then topped up with nuts and other necessary ingredients. A lot of chipmunk owners then encountered problems with feeding their pets. Fortunately, this has changed in the meantime. Manufacturers are paying more attention to correct feeding of different rodents, and some have created special squirrel feeds, which are suitable for chipmunks, but also for the European Red Squirrel, for example. Besides the usual seeds and grains, these feeds also contain walnuts, hazelnuts, dried bits of star apple, pinecone seeds, dried raisins and a number of other special ingredients for squirrels. Special squirrel food is available in pet shops. If you want to make your own food, take a mixed rodent

food without grass pellets. You add other ingredients, such as nuts, seeds and/or grains, rusk, biscuit or bread, vegetables, fruit and animal nutrients.

Nuts

Almost all nuts are suitable for chipmunks, but peanuts and walnuts are their favourites. Acorns and chestnuts are also very popular. Refrain from feeding too many nuts. They contain a lot of vitamin E, which is good for your pet's vitality, but they are also very fattening. A bit of extra fat is ok if the animal is preparing for hibernation. During the rest of the year, or if the animal is not exposed to outside temperatures, don't let it get overweight. It goes without saying that a chipmunk must never be fed salted peanuts or other salty nuts! Young animals in particular might find it difficult to open hard nuts. You can come to the rescue with a nutcracker or a hammer. Nuts are not cheap, but they will keep for quite a long time. If you see a special offer somewhere, you can therefore buy a bit more. You will find plenty of chestnuts, acorns, pinecones and hazelnuts in the autumn. You can stock up your nut supply for months with just one quick walk through the woods.

Seeds and grains

Oats, wheat, maize, corn, barley and rye are all suitable for squirrels.

Oats are nutritious and are available whole or crushed. Crushed oats are preferable, as whole oats can be quite sharp and can, in some cases, injure the inside of the pouch.

Wheat is rich in vitamin E, but a lot of animals are not very fond of it. It is, however, important that they eat it.

Corn is one of the cheapest feeds. It is rich in energy and must therefore be fed especially in winter and, in less quantity, in summer.

Maize is rich in energy, too. A lot of rodents won't touch it or will just nibble at it. It is, however, healthy and part of a balanced diet.

Sunflower seeds are very popular with any rodent. They are rich in vegetable oils and vitamin E and are thus important for your pet's health. Too many sunflower seeds cause obesity. The chipmunk needs to put on weight before hibernation, but obesity causes reproduction problems in spring. You can add some sunflower seeds to the main feed, but not too many.

You can buy seeds and grains in pet shops, supermarkets and at feed merchants'. It is often cheaper to buy a large amount in one go. Be careful, though, as most feeds lose their energy and vitamins after about three months. You can, however, get together with a few people and share a large amount of food.

Mixed seeds, grains and nuts

Rusk, biscuits and bread

Chipmunks generally like rusk, biscuits, toast and (dried) bread. This gives them something to gnaw at. Be careful with biscuits: sugar and/or salt are bad for rodents. Sugar is bad for almost all animals!

Vegetables

Vegetables are ideal chipmunk food: fresh, full of vitamins and nice and juicy.

Lettuce is especially rich in vitamins and water (95 percent) and therefore great food. Do not give more than a few leaves at once.

Cabbage is not as suitable. It has very few vitamins and can upset the intestines. The leaves and head of a cauliflower are very healthy for your chipmunk: they are very nutritious. Kale is nutritious and cheap: you can feed the whole plant. Never feed too much cabbage, though.

Chicory and endives are popular with many animals. They are inexpensive, healthy greens without disadvantages.

Although carrots are particularly nutritious and healthy, most animals do not particularly like them. Summer carrots might be accepted, but chipmunks often find the flavour of winter carrots too strong. It is worth trying whether your chipmunk likes carrots, as tastes vary!

There are plenty of other vegetables suitable for rodents. It is only a matter of trying what your pet likes. Be careful about possible insecticides. Wash vegetables properly if you are in any doubt!

Fruit

All squirrels, and thus chipmunks, too, love fruit. They'll eat anything: apples, pears, melons, grapes, bananas, plums (without stones!), peaches, oranges, strawberries, berries, etc. Remove any fruit from the cage that has not been eaten. Rotting fruit is not good for hygiene! Just as with vegetables, you should make sure that all fruit is free of insecticides.

A chipmunk will generally also enjoy dried fruit, such as mixed dried fruit, raisins and currants. Just like nuts, fruit can be either cheap or expensive: the woods are full of brambles and berries, and the supermarkets are full of exotic fruit. With a bit of work, you can save a lot of money.

Animal nutrients
In the wild, chipmunks are believed to supplement their vegetable menu with baby birds, eggs and insects. So they also need some animal nutrients in captivity. There are plenty of squirrel owners who give their pets no or very little animal matter, and still have healthy pets and good breeding results. Chipmunks seem to stay well away from birds' nests and eggs in captivity.

It is advisable, however, to give your chipmunk some animal food. This might be dried cat or dog food, boiled eggs or insects. A chipmunk likes mealworms, and, if it is housed together with birds, it will join them at their bowls of seeds and egg food. You can keep mealworms alive in a bowl, somewhere where it is not too warm. Give them a piece of fruit once in a while, preferably a bit of orange. This increases the worms' nutritional value.

Vitamins and minerals

A chipmunk hoards a lot of its food. Not everything that disappears from the feed bowl will be eaten. As long as the menu is balanced and the animal has plenty of exercise, it will not become obese and you will not have to add any vitamins or minerals. If your pet's health does need a bit of help, though, you can add some vitamins and minerals via its drink water. You can also dip the mealworms into a supplement, such as gistocal, before feeding them. Do not feed more than three to five worms a day in that case. Avoid overdosing any supplements!

A lot of fanciers offer their pets extra minerals via a mineral lick. This lick is attached to the inside of the cage, so that the animals can lick at it when they feel the need. Pregnant and lactating females in particular use licks a lot. Mineral licks can be bought in any pet shop.

Water

Squirrels need access to fresh water all the time. You can offer them water in a bowl or a drinking bottle. These bottles can be bought in various designs and sizes in pet shops. Buy a model that is easy to clean: a layer of algae tends to form in these bottles and is difficult to remove. If you offer water in a bowl, you must make sure that it cannot be tipped over.

Make sure that the water in the bottle does not freeze in winter. If it is freezing, it might be a good idea to put the water in a bowl. If your chipmunk is not hibernating and the water is frozen, it can gnaw at the ice and get its fluids that way.

Drinking bottle

Chipmunks have a very particular way of drinking. They do not drink in a licking manner like cats and dogs, but they suck the water in like horses. A chipmunk drinks approximately five millilitres a day.

Eating droppings

As vitamin B12 is not directly accessible for some rodents (including the chipmunk), it has to be produced by bacteria in the digestive tract. These animals' droppings have a fairly loose structure and contain not only partly digested food, but also vitamin B12. The animals eat these droppings. You might not find this particularly appetising, but it is very important for your chipmunk's health!

Mineral lick

Housing

In the wild, chipmunks live underground in burrows and tunnels with a nesting chamber, or in hollow tree trunks. The nest is filled with foliage for warmth.

Typically, each chipmunk pair has its own nesting area. In some species, the couples form a true community with each other.

Chipmunk burrows are intricate complexes. The entrance is normally at the base of a tree trunk, hidden between shrubs and plants. The tunnel descends at an angle of 45 degrees, and ends horizontally in a round chamber, in which the nest is situated. If there are side-passages, there are never more than three.

These burrows usually have just one exit. The length of the corridors varies from sixty centimetres to a good four metres. The chambers are twenty to forty centimetres wide and are forty centimetres to one metre under the surface. Some burrows have small corridors filled with droppings. Food is normally hoarded in chambers, sometimes in corridors. The nest is generally an open chamber with nesting material in the middle.

Choosing between indoors and outdoors

You can keep chipmunks both indoors and outdoors, as they originate in both cold and warm areas. Heat and cold do not affect them, whereas damp and draughts do. So you do not have to keep your chipmunk inside because of the climate. Whether you keep chipmunks indoors or outdoors, both have their advantages and disadvantages. The table on page 28 puts them in an overview:

You'll find 'hibernation' four times in the table. A hibernating pet has its advantages and disadvantages, too. You can read more about this in the chapter 'Behaviour'.

An animal that is kept in the open lives under more natural conditions than one kept indoors, and it is therefore more resistant to illnesses and changes in temperature. You can recognise an 'outdoor' animal by its thick, dark coat.

Pets kept outdoors are more difficult to control. They make burrows that will, eventually, be impossible for you to reach into. They are also usually shier than pets kept indoors. In the house, and particularly in the living room, the chance of vermin reaching their food is negligible. This is much more likely in an outdoor run. If your chipmunk escapes in the living room, it can usually be caught quite easily, even if it takes some effort. An animal escaping from an outdoor run can easily disappear forever.

A chipmunk can cause a lot of noise in a metal cage, especially if it develops stereotypical behaviour. This can cause a lot of nuisance in the living room. An indoor cage also needs to be cleaned more often. Most people also have more space available outdoors than indoors.

Advantages and disadvantages of keeping your chipmunk indoors / outdoors

Keeping chipmunks indoors

Advantages:
- More/more frequent contact with your pets
- No problems with vermin
- No problems with draughts
- Rain is no problem, either
- No hibernation
- Less risk of your chipmunk escaping

Disadvantages:
- Unnatural environment
- Limited space
- Noise
- You have to clean the cage more often
- Your pets are not as resilient
- No hibernation

Keeping them outdoors

Advantages:
- Natural environment
- You don't need to clean the run as often
- Hibernation
- Stronger animals
- No noise
- More space available

Disadvantages:
- Less contact with your pets
- Hibernation
- Less control over your chipmunks
- More risk of escaping
- More chance of vermin

Indoor housing

You can easily keep a chipmunk indoors. It is not smelly and it will cause very little inconvenience. You can also let it have a good run in the living room once in a while, although this can cause some trouble. Therefore, make your chipmunk as tame as possible before setting it free in the living room. Always be aware of the risk of your pet disappearing: all it needs is a very small gap. It also loves to dig, and finds flower pots ideal.

There are several types of chipmunk residences, most being either ready-made or DIY cages. Pet shops sell a variety of indoor cages. They are usually quite pricey. As a chipmunk needs a lot of space, a chipmunk cage is usually very expensive. Another disadvantage of such indoor cages, however suitable they might be, is that they are usually made of mesh or bars. A chipmunk jumping about in such a cage can create a lot of noise.

You can, of course, build a cage yourself to your own measurements and wishes. Perhaps you have an odd corner of 87 x 56 centimetres available.

Then make your cage that size! There are various ways to build a cage. The frame, for example, can be made of timber, aluminium or steel. The walls can be of mesh, wood, Perspex or glass. With this choice of material, never forget that the cage's resident will be a rodent. A chipmunk may not gnaw very quickly, but it will do it! It can gnaw its way out less easily on a smooth surface.

Outdoor housing

Keeping a chipmunk outdoors is a good alternative to the living room. There is usually more space to build a suitable run in the garden. A chipmunk is an escape artist, so the run has to be tight on all sides. Always check for possible gaps. Even if there is only one, your chipmunk will definitely find it!

A chipmunk can dig like there's no tomorrow. When we mention 'all sides', this includes the floor

too. Seal the floor hermetically with paving slabs, mesh or concrete. You can then put a good layer of soil on the ground. If possible, make a mound sixty to seventy centimetres high in one corner. Support it properly to prevent it from collapsing. Your pets will dig their burrows in this mound. The soil offers protection against the cold during hibernation. The walls of the run can be made of mesh, stone, glass and/or timber. Do not make a run entirely of mesh, as the animals need a part where they can find protection against wind and rain. Using too much glass can cause a greenhouse effect. Make the lower part of the run of solid material to prevent draughts over the ground. You can let your imagination run wild when building the run. Try to find a good balance between protection, ventilation, appearance, safety and convenience.

If possible, make the run so high that you can stand up in it. This makes it a lot easier to look after and clean out your pets. A lock, which you create with an extra door, reduces the risk of escape.

Mixed company

Not much experience has been gathered in keeping chipmunks and other animals together. It seems possible, however, to keep them with birds. Cases are known

of chipmunks sharing a cage with Chinese Quails, canaries, Java Sparrows and Zebra Finches. The animals even eat each other's food, and they don't seem to have any problems at all living together. These few good experiences are, however, not evidence enough to guarantee that keeping birds and chipmunks together will always be this successful. It remains a question of careful experimentation.

How much space does a chipmunk need?

A chipmunk on its own needs at least half to one cubic metre of space. You must bear in mind that ground space is not as important as height. A couple needs at least two cubic metres. These sizes might seem exaggerated, but that is not the case. Chipmunks are incredibly active. They also are not fond of being too close to one another: that would inevitably cause fights!

From indoors to outdoors

If you want to move your chipmunk from indoors to outdoors, keep a close watch on changes in temperature. The most suitable time for 'moving home' is between mid-May and the end of June. The animal can slowly get used to life outdoors in the summer warmth, and slowly adapt to the winter cold during autumn.

Interior

You can make the interior of the run as pretty and as exciting as you want: slides, climbing poles and maybe plants. Whether the plants will survive for long depends on the species. Chipmunks normally leave conifers alone, but they like to dig up plants with short roots. Be aware of plants with poisonous leaves and/or fruit. Eating them can be fatal for your pet! Fruit tree branches are ideal in runs. You can leave the leaves on them, but make sure the branches and leaves are free of insecticides. If in doubt, rinse them!

Hang up plenty of nesting logs, always more than there are animals. You can use some bigger birch logs. Nesting boxes are also suitable. Hang all logs at the same height. This prevents fights for the highest place. Also avoid hanging the logs too close to each other. Spread out plenty of nesting material (hay). Also put some tobacco sticks in the cage, against red mites.

Escaping

A chipmunk escape is not a big deal indoors. If it escapes outside, however, the situation is much more serious. If it is just a single chipmunk, leave its cage open. There is quite a good chance that it will return before dark. If an animal has escaped from a group of chipmunks, it is, of course, not possible to use this 'trick'. If a

couple has escaped, there is very little hope that they will return of their own free will. If they also start a family in the wild, the chipmunk becomes a native species. This is called fauna falsification. This can cause damage to indigenous animal species, such as the European Red Squirrel, and it should therefore be prevented.

Escaped animals will normally stay in the neighbourhood for a while. You can try to lure them into a trap with some of their favourite food. Or you might be able to catch them with a net.

Behaviour

Grown chipmunks can be a bit wild and shy, especially if they were caught in the wild. Young animals, which grew up at a fancier's, can be surprisingly tame.

Typical relaxed sitting position of a chipmunk.

The ground squirrel will, however, never become a cuddly toy. Chipmunks have an incredible amount of energy and are very lively. This makes them pleasant to look at and to look after.

Behaviour in the wild

To better understand your chipmunk's behaviour, it is important to know how the animal behaves in its original habitat. This will make it clear why we have to take care of these animals' special needs, and how we can make life with us resemble life in the wild as closely as possible.

The chipmunk is a diurnal animal in the wild. Its daily life seems to change a lot from season to season. It will only appear from its burrow when the sun warms the earth in spring. It will be most active between ten o'clock in the morning and four o'clock in the afternoon. It will disappear into its burrow again at dusk. If it is wet and windy, the chipmunk will stay at home.

In summer, chipmunks get up at dawn, as soon as there is enough light to see. They are very active: besides their normal feeding and mating behaviour, they go bathing and jump and chase around. They will have a nap in their burrows between twelve and two. After that, they are active again until dusk.

Chipmunks seem to be bothered far less by rain and wind in the summer and autumn than they are in the spring. This might be explained by the fact that chipmunks were observed primarily in areas where it rains a lot in these months. Another explanation might be that the rain is not so cold and therefore less unpleasant in summer and autumn.

Their behaviour in autumn is very similar to that in summer. The warm daylight is used to forage and (particularly) to build up winter reserves. As the chipmunk has such a wide distribution, winter behaviour depends very much on the dominating climate. In the coldest parts of Siberia, the animals hibernate completely from October to March. In other areas, mild weather wakes them up and lures them out of their burrows.

Swaying its tail

Sometimes a chipmunk will suddenly stand still, stick up its tail and start swaying it. This looks like a dog's wagging, but it is not as fast. The swaying is a sign of attention, and sometimes of fear. When an animal sways its tail, it is very alert and can react any moment. It is possible that a chipmunk sways its tail to appear taller and scare off possible enemies.

The chipmunk's tail is an important balancing tool. This does not mean, however, that the animal cannot survive if it ends up with half or none of its tail after an accident. It will get used to the new situation very quickly and will soon climb and jump around quite nicely again, although its performances will never again be quite the way they were.

Hoarding

All chipmunks, including the Asiatic Ground Squirrel, are true hoarders. Their Latin names *Eutamias* and *Tamias* indicate as much: they mean something like 'the true collector'. Chipmunks have enormous pouches. Scientists have recorded 'freight' of 6 chestnuts, 60 sunflower seeds, 32 beechnuts and even 13 plum stones. Especially when winter approaches, the chipmunk will create several hoards. Quantities of one to two kilos are no exception. Always let a chipmunk make its hoards. They consist of non-perishable food, such as sunflower seeds, nuts, seeds and dried fungi.

Hibernation

In the wild, it depends on the climate whether a chipmunk hibernates or not. It is basically the same in captivity. A chipmunk kept indoors will not normally hibernate, an 'outdoor' animal will. Here, too, exceptions prove the rule. Older chipmunks normally start to hibernate earlier than younger animals.

Chipmunks bury their food.

Hibernation has advantages and disadvantages. Animals that hibernate tend to live longer. They do not 'wear out' during the winter months: life just gets delayed a bit. Mating behaviour is stronger after hibernation. Hibernation has disadvantages too, however. You will not see your pet during this time. It is also more difficult to check on it. Animals can also freeze to death if they cannot tuck themselves away properly.

Hibernation can consist of a few short spells, but a chipmunk can also be gone for five to six months without you ever getting to see it. Most animals start to hibernate between October and November, depending on the weather. They will first make sure that they have enough supplies, both in their body (fat reserves) and in their burrow (food). The respiration rate during hibernation drops to approximately once per minute. The body temperature drops to just a few degrees above the temperature in the burrow.

Taming

Although the chipmunk is not a cuddly toy, and will never be one, it can still become a pleasant, tame housemate. It will always have its own will. Only chipmunks that have been raised with a bottle will become trained to the hand completely

A chipmunk must be tamed at a young age. All animals have a period when they are most responsive to outside influences. This is the most suitable moment to tame an animal. The chipmunk's 'socialisation period' is in its second month, when the young are still with the mother. The parents' owner will therefore have to initiate the taming process When the young leave the nest after about four weeks, you can begin to tame them.

You can take advantage of two very important elements of a chipmunk's life when taming it: the appeal of the chipmunk call and your pet's inquisitive nature.

Taking advantage of the chipmunk call

Chipmunks use their call particularly during the mating season, but also during the rest of the time. Both males and females react to it. Males feel attracted to it, females become inquisitive. This call sounds similar to a bird's whistling.

Offering treats

Once you have caught your pet's attention, it should then come to you. Chipmunks are inquisitive animals and will almost certainly come to see what you've got to offer. If they're not too shy, they will accept a piece of fruit, a sunflower seed, raisin, nut or mealworm from you. If they are still too scared, you can push the treat through the mesh or the bars. Slowly go back a step, until the distance is big enough for the squirrel to overcome its fear. If the treat is worth the trouble, it will accept it quicker next time. This 'trick' works better if your chipmunk is hungry. Give your pets a few days to get used to their new surroundings before you attempt to tame them. Young chipmunks hardly ever remain shy. Curiosity will win over fear, even if it takes some time and work.

Chipmunks can become very tame.

Reproduction

After some time you might have so much fun with your chipmunk(s) that you decide to breed a litter yourself.

Chipmunks happily use nesting boxes.

You do not have to pair chipmunks that live with a partner or in a group. If you keep them separate (which is actually best), you have to pair them when the female is ready to mate. You can tell this moment by the female's 'whistling': a female on heat is like a canary. The breeding season starts somewhere between December and March with animals that are kept inside. Outside, it starts after the frost and hibernation are over. The male is then fertile continuously, the female for three days every two weeks.

When the female starts to whistle, you can put your chipmunks together. Set the male to the female. If that does not work, choose a spot for pairing which is new to both animals. Mating

normally occurs quite quickly after pairing. If the female starts to behave more aggressively towards the male, it is a sign that mating has occurred. It is then time to separate the animals again.

The breeding season lasts approximately from March to September, but the peaks are in April/May and July/August.

Pregnancy and birth

A chipmunk's pregnancy lasts approximately 31 to 32 days. A little longer or shorter is quite normal, too. The mother-to-be looks no different at the beginning, but the further the pregnancy progresses, the more her appearance changes. Towards the end of the pregnancy, her enlarged teats become visible.

The female withdraws from the other chipmunks on the day of the birth. The birth normally occurs in the evening or at night. Usually, three to five young are born, but it may be any number between one and eight. There's normally an equal number of male and female babies, but there are exceptions here, too.

Most chipmunks have one litter a year. There might be a second litter, which is usually smaller than the first. Approximately three months will pass between two litters. In very exceptional cases, chipmunks that are kept inside might even have a third litter.

Development

Newly born chipmunks are like small, fat worms. They are totally helpless: naked, blind and deaf. Slowly but steadily, these worms develop into real squirrels. On the fiftieth day, they will have reached 90 percent of the length and 65 percent of the weight of grown animals. At the age of two months, the young will start to display 'sexual' behaviour: They try to mount each other, but

without success. You can also expect the youngsters to start behaving aggressively towards each other now.

Rearing by hand

It can happen that the mother of a litter dies while giving birth or shortly afterwards. It can also happen that the mother rejects one or more young. They will lie outside the nest. These young have no chance of survival on their own. You can try and rear these 'orphans' by hand. You must bear in mind that something is wrong with young that have been rejected by the mother. A mother does not abandon them for no reason. There are, however, also hand-reared young that live a long and happy life. Pets that have been reared this way will regard their carer as their mother. They will be very tame and affectionate towards him or her. A human cannot teach chipmunk characteristics and skills. This animal will thus be a bit lost in the chipmunk world and should not be used for breeding.

When a chipmunk baby loses its mother, there are two immediate threats to its life: hypothermia and starvation. A young chipmunk has to be kept warm, but must not become dehydrated. Lay it in a nest with damp cloths and don't cover it too heavily. Hang a lamp above the nest. Make sure that the young chipmunk does not dehydrate and that it cannot burn itself on the lamp.

How the young develop:

Ears erect:	approx. 7 days
Stripes visible:	approx. 11 days
Squeak up to:	approx. 14 days
Fur totally developed:	approx. 16 days
Ears and eyes open:	approx. 27 days
Leave the nest:	approx. 30 days
Weaned:	40-50 days

Weight development:

Days	Weight approx
10	10 grams
20	20 grams
30	35 grams
40	60 grams
50	75 grams
60	90 grams

To feed the baby, you have to imitate its mother's milk. You can do this with gruel, which you heat up to 37 to 38 degrees.

A healthy chipmunk baby will eat just as much as it needs. An ill animal can cause some problems. It it will not or cannot suck, you can feed it via a stomach tube, which you can make from a syringe. Put a thin tube over the nozzle and very slowly insert it. The young animal should eat at least ten percent of its own weight per day. Administer its food slowly and carefully, so that you can watch it swallow. Choking is one of the biggest hazards of artificial feeding. If bubbles appear in its nostrils, or the animal begins to cough or vomit, lift it up by its back paws, so that the fluid can drain.

Artificial feeding can also cause diarrhoea. The gruel is then probably too rich in nutrients, which the baby's stomach cannot cope with yet. Dilute the gruel and add an extra feed. Be aware of the danger of dehydration if the infant is suffering from diarrhoea. As you can see in the plan,

Young chipmunks

hand-rearing a squirrel is a day-and-night job during the first few weeks. If you want to give your pet a chance of survival, continuous care is vital. Don't miss any night feeds during the first few weeks, as the young chipmunk cannot cope without them.

After feeding, carefully massage its belly and bladder. Do this with a damp cotton bud. This massage is essential to generate faeces. It is

Composition
Chipmunk baby food:
• 3 tsp baby food (e.g. Cow and Gate, Heinz)
• 1 tsp condensed milk
• 1/2 tsp honey
Dilute with water until it is a liquid gruel. Add a little vitamin-preparation.

Number of feeds:
• 1-2 weeks every 4 hours
• 2-3 weeks every 6 hours
• 3-7 weeks every 8 hours.

of the utmost importance that you keep stimulating your pet's metabolism at this young age. A chipmunk baby will fall asleep after it has been fed.

Life expectancy
It is a fact that species that have been domesticated longer will also live longer. In general, domestication provides them with a more luxurious life-style than in the wild, and they no longer have natural enemies, or are out of their reach in the house or garden. A chipmunk's life expectancy depends to a large extent on the right diet, care and housing. As it is very much a 'newcomer' to domestication, it is difficult to

give an average life expectancy. You can assume that male animals will live no longer than eight, females no longer than twelve years.

Your chipmunk's health

Luckily, the chipmunk is quite resilient. It is not often ill and if it is not quite right, in 95 out of 100 cases this is due to incorrect care, diet or housing.

This chapter deals briefly with treatments for a number of ailments. This advice is only meant to give a short insight into the treatment required. It is not intended to encourage you to start experimenting with medicines or, worse, with a knife. Unfortunately, not all vets are familiar with chipmunks' ailments and the necessary treatments. Because they are relatively unknown, small exotic pets are still quite a novelty in many veterinary practices.

A healthy chipmunk
To be able to recognise an ill animal, you need to know what a healthy animal looks like. A healthy chipmunk is active and lively. It looks around with bright eyes and enjoys life. Its coat is smooth and shiny. A healthy chipmunk sits in a slightly 'round' posture and curls up when sleeping. It is slim without being skinny. In autumn, it needs to build up fat reserves for hibernation. At rest, a chipmunk breathes 75 times per minute. Its body temperature is 38 degrees.

Old age
The best thing that can happen to a chipmunk is a quiet, peaceful death after a long and happy life. This does not always happen in the wild, of course. Ill and old animals are easy prey for predators, because they cannot escape so quickly. Very few animals die of old age in the wild. Luckily, this is different in captivity. If a chipmunk has been looked after well all its life, and

does not become ill, it will slowly, but steadily, grow old. You can recognise an older chipmunk by its coat. It is no longer so smooth, and it is duller. The animal becomes less active and eats less. The coat will also become grey with time. When your chipmunk is old and will probably not live for much longer, you need to leave it in peace as far as you can. As long as your pet is not suffering or in pain, do nothing. If it is suffering, however, you should think about having it put to sleep.

Prevention

Prevention is better than a cure. It might sound like an old tune, but this saying applies to chipmunks, too. Even if you follow all the advice in this book, there is no guarantee that your chipmunk will not become ill. But you do reduce the chance of suffering quite considerably. Be particularly attentive when putting couples and/or groups together. Being forced to live together can lead to fights, which often end fatally.

Examination

A chipmunk does not like being picked up. It is therefore difficult to examine. Observing the animal is an important part of examination. Pay attention to how your squirrel moves. Is it limping? Is it moving strangely? If you do have to hold your chipmunk to examine it, try to

catch it in a dim environment: diurnal animals are always a little calmer in the dark. Do not forget to wear thick leather gloves, as chipmunks bite very quickly when picked up. Always beware of the risk of escape. If you are in any doubt about your chipmunk's health, a vet can examine its urine, droppings and blood.

You can have a closer look at your chipmunk when it is hanging onto the mesh.

Bite wounds

If something is wrong with your chipmunk, in eight out of ten cases it is the result of a fight. As already mentioned, chipmunks live solitary lives in the wild, and living together in a limited space is an unnatural situation. If you keep chipmunks in pairs or groups, you must expect fights, which are usually quite serious. Always pay attention! Bite wounds normally heal quickly, as long as they are not too serious. But it is quite possible for a chipmunk to die of the injuries it has sustained in a fight. A lot of these little hooligans run around with plenty of scars. Ears and tails in particular will suffer. If bite wounds are so serious that they won't heal within a few days or need stitching, you need to take the victim to the vet's. He will stitch the wound and, if necessary, treat the animal with antibiotics. It is obvious that a squirrel does not like bandaging, so this won't normally be done.

In general

An ill chipmunk is far less lively than usual. Its eyes might be dull and its coat tangled. If it is sitting listlessly in a corner and not eating, there is definitely something wrong. Remember hibernation! A hibernating chipmunk is also less active and won't touch its food. Warmth and rest will help when treating almost any ailment. Try and find out quickly if the illness is contagious, and bear your other pets in mind. If the illness is not contagious, it is better not to separate the animals, as this can cause big problems when you want to put them back together again later.

Fractures

Broken bones are nearly always the result of incorrect care. A healthy squirrel, which sits in a good cage and is handled correctly, won't break anything. Most broken bones are caused by an inadequate cage interior, being dropped, picked up by the tail, transported wrongly, things falling over in the cage or other external influences. A fracture can be difficult to diagnose. If the animal is moving with difficulty or strangely, or is less active, it might be a fracture. Only a vet has the experience and the equipment (x-ray machine) to diagnose a fracture. A fracture can hardly ever be put in a splint. You must limit the animal's exercise as much as possible, so that the fracture can heal. Keep your chipmunk in a small cage in dim, cool surroundings that are as quiet as possible.

Skin conditions

There are three types of skin conditions that can affect a chipmunk: fungal infections, skin inflammations and skin conditions caused by parasites.

Fungal infections

A beginning fungal infection causes small scales between the hairs. It will first become visible on the ears and around the nose. Later on, the skin will become scabby and crusts will form. Fungal infections are not dangerous in themselves, but the itching can cause the animals to scratch themselves until they bleed. This will cause inflammations, which can become very serious. Another problem with fungal infections is that they are highly contagious, sometimes even for humans! These types of infection therefore require preventative measures: isolate the infected chipmunk immediately and be very rigorous in terms of hygiene (always wash your hands

after contact with the infected animal). Check other chipmunks for fungal infections, too. Clean out the infected animal's cage properly. Your vet will prescribe a preparation to treat the infection.

Skin inflammations

A small wound or a splinter, for example, can cause a skin inflammation. If such an inflammation is underneath the skin, and the skin heals on the surface, a small lump will develop. This is called an abscess. Abscesses can also have other causes, such as in-breeding, for example. Such bacterial inflammations need to be treated by a vet. If necessary, he will cut it open and clean it out. Never open an abscess yourself! It must

be done in a sterile environment with sterile instruments!

Skin inflammations are treated with antibiotics. There are hundreds of different types, which fight all sorts of different bacteria. The type of bacteria must first be determined with a culture. Then the vet can prescribe the correct antibiotic. Until then, the animal is given a so-called 'antibiotic cocktail'.

Parasites

Chipmunks do not normally carry parasites. This does not rule out, however, that an individual cannot become infested by parasites such as (red) mites, fleas and ticks. Ill and weak animals in particular are popular prey for parasites.

Sleeping in the sun

Lice can actually only survive in a badly cared-for coat. Ill, weak and undernourished animals are very susceptible.

Mites cause an untidy, irregular coat. Dandruff can form on parts of skin without hair. Mites can also cause eczema. They feed on the animal's skin discharge (scabs, etc.). Mites can seriously weaken young chipmunks in particular.

Red mites are a 'secretive' infestation. They look like tiny white spiders. When they have filled up, they become red. Red mites are extremely contagious. Ask your vet for a preparation to fight them. Tobacco sticks in the cage and nesting logs reduce the risk of red mites significantly.

Fleas suck blood from their host animal, like on dogs and cats. They can reproduce very quickly (as most parasites). A chipmunk with lots of fleas can suffer from allergies and/or inflammations. The itching might cause the animal to scratch or bite itself until it bleeds.

Ticks, too, suck blood. A tick lets itself drop onto an animal or human and burrows itself into the fur. It bites into the skin with its jaws and won't let go. The rear fills up with blood and can become as big as a pea. Ticks can cause serious illnesses. Grab a tick behind the head with tweezers and pull it out of the skin with a clockwise movement. It is inadvisable to 'numb' the tick

with alcohol or oil beforehand, as it might empty its toxic stomach contents into the host animal in a shock reaction. Check that the head hasn't remained in the skin, as this can cause infections. Disinfect the spot where the tick was. Have a vet remove any head that has remained in the skin.

Elephant's teeth

When a rodent's incisors do not wear down as they should, a condition called 'elephant's teeth' develops. The teeth of rodents, rabbits and hares grow continuously, because they get worn down so quickly by their gnawing. The teeth should normally fit onto each other properly.

A tooth's growth speed normally adapts naturally to the distance to the opposite tooth. A fall, an impact or not enough gnawing opportunities can make a tooth stand at an odd angle. There is no longer an opposite tooth, which means that the tooth can grow into the opposite jaw unrestrained. The animal can no longer close its mouth and the whole jaw is damaged, with nasty consequences for the animal.

Rodents' teeth can be cut back, rasped or ground down. It is therefore very easy to help a chipmunk with elephant's teeth. The condition will practically always return. It may happen after a few months, or a few years. You can delay it by feeding your pet lots of hard feed. Let it gnaw a lot. The symptoms of elephant's teeth are: dribbling, a wet chin and/or chest, lack of appetite, loss of weight, only using one side of its jaw, an inflamed jaw and/or apathy. As squirrels are very quick and do not like to be caught, take them to the vet's if you suspect elephant's teeth. Elephant's teeth can be hereditary. Therefore, never breed with an animal suffering from a dental abnormality.

Diarrhoea
Diarrhoea is usually the consequence of intestinal illness. Intestinal illnesses can have various causes. It is not always easy to diagnose diarrhoea with chipmunks, but you must watch out for it. Young animals, in particular, can dehydrate quickly and die as a consequence.

Your vet can prescribe the right medicine after a simple laboratory test. If the diarrhoea is not serious, feed your pet dry bread, rusk or some toast. Add a bit of rose-hip syrup to its drinking water. It is very important that diarrhoea doesn't go on for days.

Colds and pneumonia

Chipmunks should never catch colds or pneumonia under normal circumstances. Even the strongest chipmunk, however, might become a victim: If it is transferred from indoors to outdoors at the wrong time of the year, is subjected to bad ventilation, draughts, damp, or because it has become infected by its cage-mates.

You can recognise colds and pneumonia by a chipmunk's strained breathing. Sometimes, discharge comes from the nose. The animal looks ill: It sits hunched up and has a messy coat. An animal with a respiratory problem needs to be taken to the vet as quickly as possible, as it needs to be treated with antibiotics. Make sure that other animals cannot be infected.

Stereotypical movements

Squirrels need a lot of exercise. If they do not have enough room to exercise, they can develop behavioural disorders. One of the most common abnormalities is the development of stereotypical movements. A certain movement may be repeated for hours.

Squirrels will usually run around the same circle for hours. Once an animal has developed this behaviour, it will not normally stop again. Therefore, provide your pets with a spacious home and plenty of distraction. This prevents boredom and thus stereotypical behaviour.

Post-mortem

Whenever a pet dies, it is a very sad occasion. Despite all the emotions, you have to remain sensible: it is important to find out what killed the animal. This is particularly important to be able to protect other pets against contagious diseases. It is also important to prevent possible mistakes in care, feeding or caging from happening again.

Could it have been a viral or bacterial infection? Are other animals infected? Has a mistake been made in its care? Has the animal eaten bad food or something poisonous? Has it been fed incorrectly or has something else killed it? A vet can answer all these questions with a post-mortem report. If you only had one pet, there is not such a big need to answer all these questions. If you have several pets, a fast post-mortem can save lives.

During a post-mortem, the dead animal will be cut open and its organs examined. The contents of its stomach and its blood and

urine will be examined. In 95 percent of cases, a post-mortem can determine the cause of death. If a viral or bacterial infection killed your chipmunk, the post-mortem will provide the necessary information to choose the right medication to treat any other animals.

In some cases, your vet will be able to do the post-mortem, but in most cases the animal will have to be sent to a laboratory for veterinary science.

A post-mortem should be done soon after the animal died. It is best to take the carcass to the laboratory yourself, but you can also send it by post. If, for some reason, you cannot send the carcass straight away, put it in the freezer for a while. This will conserve the animal as far as possible. However, not all tests can be carried out if too much time has passed.

Looking for more information

Chipmunk
(Tamias striatus)

Squirrels are generally not easy to keep as pets. The chipmunk is a little more easy-going, but it is pretty difficult to feed and look after other squirrel species in a correct and responsible manner. It is therefore very important that you collect all the necessary information about the pet you are planning to keep. You can then decide on the basis of this information whether the animal you are intending to get is the right one for you. Never buy a pet if you are in any doubt!

Especially as far as exotic pets are concerned, it is not always easy to get access to information. It can even be difficult to find out where to begin with your search. This chapter is an attempt to show you the right way.

Libraries

Apart from the organisations, mentioned on pages 60 to 61 you will have to rely on books if you are looking for information about squirrels. Public libraries have a variety of books about common animal species. If you are interested in a specific animal or want to look at a topic in more depth, you will have to depend on scientific publications. You will find these publications in the libraries of universities or museums. These libraries are generally not open to the public, but you can often ask to look at specific titles. It depends on the individual libraries how far they will assist you in your search. It is always helpful to know what you are looking for in advance. If possible, take a list with titles and authors with you, as this can save a lot of time and trouble.

Zoos

In special cases, you can ask knowledgeable zoo employees for help. They are, of course, not prepared for hoards of people appearing with questions about their pets, and in most cases they will refer these people to the organisations mentioned later in this book. A specific question or an interesting case can, however, be interesting for a zoo too.

Himalayan striped squirrel
(Tamias macclellandi)

Chipmunk
(Tamias striatus)

Tricolor squirrel
(C allosciurus prevosti)

Chinese striped squirrel
(Tamias swinhoei)

African ground squirrel

Prairydog

Grey squirrel

European squirrel

Tips

- Isolate the victim of a contagious disease!
- Let your chipmunk have its run before feeding time. You can then lure it back into the cage with some food.
- Beware of possible insecticides.
- Wash fruit and vegetables if in any doubt.
- One chipmunk in a cage causes far less trouble than a couple or a group.
- A chipmunk on its own is not unhappy; unless its cage is too small!
- Use a solid box to transport your chipmunk.
- A chipmunk calms down in the dark.
- It is easy to determine its sex when a chipmunk is walking over, or hanging onto, mesh.
- If you have a chipmunk, it is almost certainly an Asian Chipmunk.
- When going to the vet's, take some of your pet's droppings.
- Prevent in-breeding, not just with squirrels, but also with other pets!
- Catching a chipmunk causes a lot of agitation and stress. Try luring the animal into a 'trap'.
- Animals that hibernate have a more natural biorhythm.
- Be careful when feeding artificially. Prevent choking.

- Remove any rotting food from the cage, as it can cause illnesses.
- Make sure that feed and water bowls cannot be tipped over.
- Draughts, damp, rotting or wrong food, too small a home and keeping too many animals in too small a space are all things which can endanger your chipmunk's health. Prevent them.
- Mealworms are a real treat for chipmunks.
- Give your chipmunk the opportunity to hoard food.
- Rabbit food is not suitable for chipmunks, as it contains substances that can upset small rodents' intestines.
- The bigger your chipmunk's cage, the better!
- When a female whistles, she is ready for mating.

Addresses

One can learn a lot from looking or studying other rodents or mammals. Our Siberian squirrel is a rodent that still lives in several natural habitats. Therefore knowledge of these and similar habitats can be handy as well.

Working for wildlife

We have nothing to ad to the words of "Working for Wildlife": "Working for Wildlife relies on support from members of the public. You can directly support the wildlife on the reserves by becoming a Working for Wildlife supporter or donor".

Their mission statement "Working for Wildlife aims to reverse the dramatic attrition of British wildlife and the exploitation of its habitats by promoting conditions for both to flourish while also providing access opportunities to the public for both leisure and education" is among others achieved by "Sympathetic management of, and research into, wildlife and the environment, in particular sites of special scientific and/or historical interest, where animals live free from all forms of cruelty.

Education and the promotion of best practice in wildlife conservation, principally through the internet, schools, promotional literature and sanctuary sites. Providing opportunities for the public to view wildlife at close quarters at appropriate sites, without adversely affecting the best interests of the wildlife."

Working for Wildlife
83-87 Union Street
London
SE1 1SG
Phone: 0207 089 5201
Fax 0207 378 6940
e-mail:
info@workingforwildlife.org.uk

RSPCA

Since 1824 the Society for the Prevention of Cruelty to Animals - the (R)SPCA has worked to promote kindness to animals and has tried to prevent cruelty to animals.

Already in 1822 a bill was piloted through parliament: cattle, horses and sheep got a degree of protection. Queen Victoria gave her permission to the SPCA to call themselves Royal Society for the Prevention of Cruelty to animals (RSPCA) in 1840. By this time the Society's work was held in high regard.

RSPCA
Wilberforce Way
Southwater
Horsham
West Sussex RH13 9RS

Phone: 0870 33 35 999 (or +44 870 33 35 999 for calls from outside the UK). The enquiries service is open Monday to Friday, 9am to 5pm.
Fax: 0870 75 30 284 (or +44 870 75 30 284 from outside the UK) to the enquiries service at RSPCA headquarters.

Cotswold Wildlife park

On their website you see information about the *Tamias Sibiricus* or Siberian Chipmunk. So make a call for opening times and go have a look. A visit to the zoo always makes a great day!

Cotswold Wildlife Park
Burford
Oxfordshire
United Kingdom
OX18 4JW
Phone: +44 (0) 1993 823006

The Mammal Society

The Mammal Society is "The only organisation solely dedicated to the study and conservation of all British mammals.

Their mission statement is: "The Mammal Society works to protect British mammals, halt the decline of threatened species, and advise on all issues affecting British Mammals. We study mammals, identify the problems they face and promote conservation and other policies based on sound science"

Among others they seek to: "Promote mammal studies in the UK and overseas; Provide current information on mammals through our publications; Educate people about British mammals; Monitor mammal population changes".

The Mammal Society
2B, Inborth Street
London SW11 3EP
Phone: 020 7350 2200
Fax: 020 7350 2211

The chipmunk on the internet

A great deal of information can be found on the internet. A selection of websites with interesting details and links to other sites and pages is listed here. Sometimes pages move to another site or address. You can find more sites by using the available searchmachines.

www.borealforest.org
A Canadian site about Mammal Species of the World's Boreal Forests and with detailed information about the Siberian chipmunk. All about the distinguished features, its habitats and the trees it favours. All about their cleaning and grooming each other and a lot more.

www.rspca.org.uk
On this site you can find all about the RSPCA, the advice centre, there is lots of news. Find out all about their campaigns, about animal care, rehoming, education and a lot more.
The website is open for your registration. The RSPCA values your opinion. Find out how you can help.

www.workingforwildlife.org.uk
Wonderful site explaining all about their mission, trustees, links, site maps, footage from the reserves, and ecology of key species. You find information about a.o. badgers, deer, foxes, hedgehogs, otters, rabbits, hares and squirrels.

www.squirrelwerb.co.uk
A great site with lots of pictures. Basic baby squirrel care (of

orphaned grey squirrels). The site shows an interesting article about Siberian Chipmunks in four free living populations in Belgium. A load of information about our national environment and squirrel life and forestry research. There are interesting articles, a gallery and external info.

www.paw-talk.net

Paw-talk pets forum, exotics and other exotics. Description, differences with native chipmunks. What kind of pet is a chipmunk? Choosing a chipmunk, bonding, housing and feeding.

www.altpet.net

The site of the National Alternative Pet Association, who are promoting responsible private and commercial ownership of exotic animals.
The website contains: "Exotic Pet Care Info, Free Exotic Pet Adoption/Placement Listings, Exotic Pet Rescue Networking, Education of owners, breeders, pet shops, lawmakers, rescue groups, etc. Gathering information for state, county or city legalisation efforts concerning exotics, keeping an eye on exotic pet legislation, exotic pet vet referral, exotic pet breeders listing, exotic animal bookstore…" and more!!

www.sugarbushsquirrel.com

This site from the United States is not likely to show up in this list. Not everybody is charmed by dressed animals, but the wonderful pictures on this site of the Siberian Chipmunk called Sugar Bush do show a lot of patience, a tremendous amount of work and love for this animal. Beautiful pictures!

www.abdn.ac.uk

Interesting site with many interesting links, lovely pictures. Find the local organisation near your home. They are easy to contact by mail as well.

www.pethealthcare.co.uk

At Pethealthcare.co.uk they tell you that a healthy pet is a happy pet. Which is why leading experts are brought together to create a comprehensive online source of pet care information.

www.mypetstop.com

An international, multilingual website with information on keeping, breeding, behaviour, health related issues and much more.

www.aboutpets.info

The website of the publisher of the About Pets book series. An overview of the titles, availability in which languages and where in the world the books are sold.

The chipmunk

Name:	Asian or Siberian Chipmunk
Alternative name:	Asiatic Ground Squirrel
Latin name:	*Eutamias sibericus*
Origin:	North and Central Asia
Length of body:	13-19 cm
Length of tail:	8-12 cm
Weight:	75-125 grams
Fertile:	after 9 months
Pregnancy:	31-32 days
Number of young:	1-8 (average 3-5)

the **Chipmunk**